THINGS WILL GET WORSE

THINGS WILL GET WORSE

Poems by Peter Junker

Kudzu Leaf Press

Marietta, Georgia

Kudzu Leaf Press
P.O. Box 2076
Marietta, Georgia 30061
kudzuleafpress@gmail.com

kudzuleafpress.com

Copyright 2019 by Peter Junker
First edition

All rights reserved. Except in the case of brief quotations for critical articles and reviews, no part of this book may be reproduced or transmitted in any form or by any means, electronic or mechanical, including photocopying, recording, or any information storage or retrieval system, without permission in writing from the publisher. Please address permission requests to kudzuleafpress@gmail.com or Kudzu Leaf Press, P.O. Box 2076, Marietta, GA 30061.

Front cover: Design element vectors by Svetlana Kononova; English Garden font by Jim Spiece, based on typography from the book *A Flower Wedding* (1905) decorated by Walter Crane.

Poem titles are set in English Garden. The body typeface is Book Antiqua.

Author photo: Dianne Kim

ISBN: 978-0-9995304-7-4 - Paperback
eISBN: 978-0-9995304-9-8 - ePub
eISBN: 978-1-7334491-0-6 - mobi

Printed in the United States of America   102819

This paper meets the requirements of ANSI/NISO Z39.48-1992 (Permanence of Paper)

for Julie

CONTENTS

1 TALLY

On Pine Mountain in Late Summer	3
Father and Son	4
A Search	5
Biopic	6

2 YOU HEAR VOICES

Hypomania	9
Mania	10
Mood Swing, A Cold Front	11
Pity Not	12
Bless My Heart	13
A Mixed Episode	14
Friction	15
The Moment	16

3 WHAT WE'VE SEEN, LIKE SNOW

The Intake	19
The Work	20
Say Why You're Here	21
Exiles	22
Cafeteria	23
Mary Beth	24

Jemaine	25
Memory Loss	26
The Optimist	27

4 STABILITY

Stability	31
Against Epiphany	32
Against Pessimism	33
Résumé	34
Expectations	35
July, Dekalb County, Georgia	36
Heritage Hills	37
Moon	38
The Right Therapist	39
Letting Go	40
O Baklava!	41
Old-Fashioned Postcard	42
Nocturne	43

5 THE LAST SIX GUYS

For Traveling Mercies	47
Two Kinds of Vikings	48
Morning Camp on a River Bank	49
Petticoat	50
Sex Education	51

Grasshopper	52
Neighbor Ed Carithers, R.I.P.	53

6 STEEL ONESELF

Old Mill Town	57
The Man Outside Eden	58
In Barrow County, Georgia	59
Exodus 19:12	60
Life of Saint Patrick	61
Husband of the Mother of the Son of God	62
On the Neighbor's Carport Roof	63
Steel	64

7 THE EDGES OF HER

Swifty the Snow Man	67
Crisis	68
Yards of the Month	69
Unrequited 1	70
Unrequited 2	71
Rationale	72
A Near Miss	73
But Then Again	74
Forget Ulysses	75

8 BOXING UP MY STUFF

Two Become One	79
It	80
The Mugs	81
Walking Home	82
Judgment	83
Listening on a Bad Day	84
Pitty-Pat	85
Forgiveness	86
Picture Yourself	87

9 WEIRDER WITH AGE

Lives of Their Own	91
We've Come a Long Way	92
Stigma	93
Opportunity for Advancement	94
A Complainer's Complaint	95
The Predestination Paradox	96
Men's Group: M	97
Men's Group: R	98
Men's Group: D	99

10 THE MESSAGE OF SLICK PATHS

Fall Car Show	103
Blessings, by Night	104

Lightning as a Poem	105
Advice for Eve and Adam	106
NOTES	109
ACKNOWLEDGMENTS	111

Whistling to keep up courage is no mere figure of speech.
—WILLIAM JAMES

1
TALLY

ON PINE MOUNTAIN IN LATE SUMMER

Coming down Pine Mountain, a white-tail doe
Stopped me with her eyes. We watched each other
Until I felt wrong in the long silence,
Feeding on her presence. Francis, the saint,

Came to mind, preaching to birds. So I said,
"The kingdom of God is here!" I told her,
"Spread the word!" She hitched her head up and down.
She sprang when I turned away. I had to

Break camp soon and learn to live a new life,
Watched by my words coming down Pine Mountain.

FATHER AND SON

He's in his 90s, and everything hurts.
I'm halfway through a 30-year mortgage
In a green niche of DeKalb County. He's
Out west, in a brown-stucco stopover

Called assisted living. I live for love
Of my long-sought soulmate and our leafy
Home. His childhood sweetheart, my mother,
Is in hospice. He eats just enough to

Spare her the pain of him going first.
I have to prune the trees before the next frost.

A SEARCH

Regardless of the colors the valley's
Inhabitants chose to wear that morning,
Everything is stained with saturated
Clay when the mudslide comes. At first light, a

Search begins, then, *recovery* — not as
If the woodsy slopes can be reclaimed
Or bodies set to their errands again —
It's necessary to tally losses

And find safer ground. It's essential to
Acclimate to the transformed scenery.

BIOPIC

First let's exaggerate the poet's pain
To make a statement against pain and to
Make the poet a more sympathetic
Character, one we like for all that ache

Or whom we despise, but forgive, because
Of the one poem that we think we like.
Let's exhume all the childish fits of spleen,
The simmering drunk-at-the-party scenes

And the foreseeable philandery
So ill-fated we go gaga for more.

2
YOU HEAR VOICES

HYPOMANIA

My sight swells to take in the taller parts
Of God's and godlike local works —
Maples, architecture, and crisscrossed skies
Fill me with joy, as things that make sense do.

Shapes sharpen. My edges soften. At last,
Reason merges with creative insight.
My so-called work product is inspired. I'm
Emerson's own transcendent son, at one

With Nature, so in love with life that my
Life could never wear a mean appearance.

MANIA

My genius glares from the rotting wood deck.
My wit is a splinter and sledgehammer.
I'm the mockingbird, I'm the hoarse motor
Of my neighbor's weed whacker, I'm the blue-

Hot coils of my next neighbor's bug zapper.
My logic mulches from curb to hedge. My
Plans are so vast, all will see their vastness.
The termites, the clover mites, the crabgrass,

The fire ants, the mole crickets, the fungi,
All cower in my chronic real estate.

MOOD SWING, A COLD FRONT

Listen, I need to say something about
Life, and how it feels to break like a cloud
When the pressure zones instigate a brawl
And you get shoved through mountainous terrain

Until you rise, spiraling, giddy, and
Forget the picturesque lake you came from.
In the cold, you find yourself to cling to
And your self is too much to bear. You fall,

Drop by drop, on whatever chance matter
Cares or doesn't care to catch you. That's all.

PITY NOT

The sparkly, well-coiffed doctor on *Today*
Spoke first of insomnia's commonness,
So get over yourself, then cataloged
Its bloody busload of consequences,

So wake up. As for me, it lacked romance
Not to nod to the great sleepless poets
Nor note how Jesus had his eyes open.
Pity not us pooped ones. We got daylight

Should we need it. Something that some thing says
Is that something soon may reach its zenith.

BLESS MY HEART

Prednisone keeps me breathing. Ativan
Mitigates meetings. Lithium helps
Prevent catastrophes. I've grown pastry
Faced — my eye pits look filled with purple jam.

My collar asphyxiates. My gait apes
A dumb brute's. The boss, concluding I am
Moonlighting as a herd of cattle and
Idling hours in a lead mine, pulls the pin,

Citing my dearth of goods. Just as well. It's
A full-time job to comfort the concerned.

A MIXED EPISODE

Quiet enough to hear gasps coming from
A sarcophagus. The mind's fingernail
Tries incising smiles onto soap bubbles.
Reveille's called by an unseen trumpet.

Atrophied passions convulse. A sluggard
Finally lifts his hand from a poisoned
Candy bowl, exsanguinated veins filled
With cold kerosene. Credit limit reached:

The frenzied spending ends. Once-trusted gut
Tightens, impatient for the next nothing.

FRICTION

A mob is in the street outside your house.
Ions stirred by your stocking feet attach
Their polar charge as you pace, wondering
What to do when whatever it is snaps

Inside the mob outside on your front porch.
Your breath stutters. Thoughts stumble. This is fear.
With no signal but rage, the mob rushes
Your door. They are inside. You hear voices.

He's here somewhere! Let's get the bastard!
Finally, the shock — someone touches you.

THE MOMENT

And to think you thought life would be too short
When in fact the fog bank you wander through
Seems to stretch on forever. Denied
The privilege of seeing what's behind

Or ahead of you, living in the moment
Isn't all it's cracked up to be. Maybe
You'll get a do-over, per Karma, and
Come back happy as a clam in his shell,

Patient, still tender, but armored. Maybe
You'll learn to ride the tides without breaking.

3
WHAT WE'VE SEEN, LIKE SNOW

THE INTAKE

Bruised, but not so chastened that I can't hate
The fake-homey office of the intake
Nurse, its lace doilies and hangings amassed
Like quilted insults — I'm a suicide,

Not an idiot. I can see the choice,
The catch and the cave, in all her questions.
I can agitate. Or go underground.
Do you want to harm yourself or others?

I could say yes, please, but she won't get it.
I sign the papers but don't go comfy.

THE WORK

Sunday, some guy gives you the tour. You sleep.
Monday morning, meet the shrink. Remember
To speak. Tuesday, slip out of group—to sleep.
In Wednesday's meeting, the routine begins

To click. Sit in the circle. Say why you're
Here. Listen without comment to the man
With homicidal feelings for his wife
And work to stay awake till it's your turn.

At night you line up with your new pals for
The paper cup with colored seeds of light.

SAY WHY YOU'RE HERE

There are two true stories, the one telling
How the first hospital botched my mainline,
Overlacing the juice with uncountered
Corticosteroids to thin my thick lungs,

Knowing or not knowing that a knot of
Manic vim could unloose on moody me.
Arguably, the stripe, psychotic, made
A crack where the demon seeped. The other

Story starts with a kid who lost something
So precious that he learned to like to lose.

EXILES

Nobody wants to know what we know. Snow
Melts erratically and is not pretty
When come its gray crust and cavities. True,
God's view isn't our view: It counts the roil

Of maggots equal to cumulus and
A day's ooze of slush as dear as silver.
Doubt it and you're as duped as Judas, who
As far as we know was our last confrere

To truly see a paycheck from the Lord.
What we've seen, like snow, nobody's buying.

CAFETERIA

Ripsnorts crackle from the Cokeheads' table.
Further in, we melancholy Attempts
Softly share our mistakes. Not enough pills;
Mom walked in; freaked out loading the pistol.

One (call her Sylvia) tried twice to smoke
A Cadillac's tailpipe. Cleopatra
Herself would mislay an asp in this sad
Troop, yet even she might live to see Fate's

Therapeutic unmasking: Destiny
Didn't put us here; our failures save us.

MARY BETH

She says Maria is her middle name
Is why. I should give her my shirt, she says,
The tattoo-style tee-shirt with the bleeding
Heart of Mother Mary, in whose power

Yo confió. It would look good on her,
She says, and we both pretend her flirting
Conveys some magic of a charm retrieved
From before the meth, before her father

Bugged out, leaving her alone in a house
With "that bitch" in their "bumpkin town."

JEMAINE

Jemaine, the comedian, insulted
The less belligerent among us,
Walking the line between bullying
And brotherly love, before he started

Puking his meds. I asked him once, at lunch,
What it's like when the schizophrenia
Takes over. *It's like the world's blamin' me*
He said. *I hear sirens yellin' my name –*

Just like your momma last night. One night we
Heard him howling, being lugged out, witless.

MEMORY LOSS

When you reach rock bottom, it makes sense to
Dust off artifacts of higher times, but
Mementoes won't make the rent, not without
The pawn shop's help. And so I offered up

A cache of trivia, mid-way through the
Volleys of shocks I prayed would purge my bleak
Nostalgia — a comics collection,
A clarinet, some commemorative

Olympic pins, a too-small gold ring — to
Pay some bills and gamble on a clean break.

THE OPTIMIST

I will behave as though I could not hurt
The ones I love, and when it is too late,
Have sufficient stones to own it. I'll confess,
My hate of me has soaked its thin bandage

And soon may swamp us, my love. Now illness,
Loss and guilt endureth, but the gravest
Disease is love withheld. It's healed, I swear.
The bankruptcy will pass, and the children

Come back, when the time's right, with older tears.
Who wouldn't opt for more regrets than fears?

4
STABILITY

STABILITY

Fifteen years it took us to find this place,
A right-sized place, manageable debt, the
Right meds and the right therapist, the shrink
On my wife's health plan. I sit in zazen,

Take my omegas and probiotics.
One cup of coffee is ideal. I sleep
Eight hours, nine out of ten days. A check comes
Once a month. We know that things will get worse.

No one's life is easy, she reminds me.
She encourages me to write bravely.

AGAINST EPIPHANY

None of my epiphanies ended well.
It took all these years to imagine hope
As more than a side effect of naïve
Optimism. I don't buy the lightning

That knocks one on one's can, redirecting
The Self instantly forever. I'm down
Already. There are no golden tickets.
Alchemists of old weren't seeking riches:

They labored to transform sin to wisdom.
Initiation was their lot in life.

AGAINST PESSIMISM

If it's the belief that, on balance, things
Will hurt more tomorrow or the next day,
The question is, when do you stop counting?
Like if a tree falls in the forest and

No one is there to see it, how do you
Know no one is there to see it? It all—
Everything—depends. Not one of us knows
The exact moment a dying sun will

Go supernova—you presume the going.
You suffer not-knowing until the end.

RÉSUMÉ

Objective: Work with opportunity
For perfection, with ultimate
Goal of not cashing out anytime soon.
Experience: Director, Corporate

Despair; Damage Vendor; Absent Parent.
Recognition: Best Performance by a
Depressed Man in a Suit; Twice voted Most
Precarious Husband; Electroshock

Patient of the Year. Training: Certified
Straw Grasper, Institute for Sturdy Men.

EXPECTATIONS

If you do all you need to do to know
Yourself, kiss goodbye your other hobbies.
The mystery is, you'll know what you need
No matter what you've resolved. It's enough

To be one half of a conversation.
More than enough time has passed for you to
Understand the upside of *nothing lasts
Forever* – even a mood has its moods.

Better to be a patient slug than a
Professional patient. Rise. Shine, or don't.

JULY, DEKALB COUNTY, GEORGIA

It's the humidity that lends our green
Distance the opaque, shimmering edges
Of grease on a spoon. It's the near-absence
Of straight roads that makes some wandering both

Needful and romantic. It's azalea
Blooming magenta that gives a good name
To gaudy, and the slopes of each square mile
That turn passing showers into rivers.

When the wind blunders through, it's as the Lord
Said, a visit from the Holy Spirit.

HERITAGE HILLS

Being all white for now, our neighborhood's
Divide is not skin, but seed times — roughly
Fifty years it took for the turnover
From the young families who pioneered

Their beloved suburban stakes, to now, when
We newcomers outnumber the widows
Who have clearly let things go. I respect
Their privacy. The conditions of their

Kitchens and bathrooms are impossible
To know. Their floor plans are predictable.

MOON

The fountain of spirit-water. Woman
Energy. A ledger of longings.
Permission to lose ourselves in passion,
To let the same goddess who motivates

Oceans provoke us to join in the nymph
And satyr dance — lunacy, it's called.
Don't mind the melancholy that's killing
Time in the moon shadows. Its day will come —

Some dog-day noon will waste the Peace Rose blooms.
It can't touch the night-flowering jasmine.

THE RIGHT THERAPIST

Forecast says we'll be having some weather.
The leading edge of breeze has just started
To disturb the leaves on the tall hardwoods.
I'm adrift in a dandelion sea

When Phil calls. I see his face on my screen.
"Pete, how are you?" "Well," I say, "I'll tell you,
I'm in the back yard watching my poodle
Take a leak and waiting for the wind chimes."

"Oh, let me call you back later," he says,
"I didn't realize you were in church."

LETTING GO

I can explain the presence of seven
Unrestored typewriters in my attic.
I'm purging the need to set yesteryear's
Keys aright. Seven indicates a pattern, if not

Obsession—obsession, an addiction
To thoughts, thoughts slapping like the slap
Of type on paper. Nostalgia makes us
All addicts. I'm preparing to throw dead

Weight off my lifeboat to kick the habit,
To write every day anew, someday soon.

O BAKLAVA!

Walnuts, thank you for your sinewy meats,
For oil fragrant with the shadows of loam
Deeply dug and turned. Honey, oversweet
Fusion of nectars, thank you for the sting

On my tongue sparked by the amber summer
Light of your viscous liquor. Phyllo, you
Do for my avid teeth what my lover
Does atop a thrust—ceding, not yielding—

Your untold layers like tales of Turkish
Alchemists. We honor your summoning.

OLD-FASHIONED POSTCARD

Paul, There was mist on Atlanta today,
March 14, and except for the redbud
Whose color you once asked me to describe,
All the late-waking world looked far away.

I thought of you and your bride, under white
In Ann Arbor, and had to write to say
That today I seeded a cleared weed patch
With alyssum and irises. I'll get

The test for syphilis Tuesday so I
Can get married. Bliss—that's a redbud bloom.

NOCTURNE

Night draws out our themes. Slow breaths wave like wings
To keep us aloft, hovering above
Our private depths. Our sheets shush now and then,
Counseling patience to our shifting limbs.

Now and then the boy bumps against his wall
And makes a satisfied hum. Now and then
The baby offers in jagged song some
Prayer recalled from the archaic tongue.

The settling house tells of previous lives
As huts and caves. Outside, an owl hoots praise.

5
THE LAST SIX GUYS

FOR TRAVELING MERCIES

How the rodeo cowboy prays, his horse
Rocking, either unaware or pious
Beneath him, in at the microphone and
Out of the fairground loudspeakers, and through

A passing cloud of dust, and, sent from some
Ghost gland in the crowd's bowed head, it travels
To the god who gave dominion over
These quarterhorses, calves and bulls to men

Who rile and ride them because their fathers
Did: *Help us cowboys safely home.* Amen.

TWO KINDS OF VIKINGS

The settlers in Iceland learned from the lash
Of short growing seasons the ways of wild
Roots and game. Starvation called them beyond
The medieval niceties of stock,

Fodder, and private huts. When they huddled
More, fewer died. In Greenland, though, the Norse
Held fast the post walls. Grave-work wasted thaws
As the rigid Viking rank diminished.

They left a square church — odd to the migrant
Inuit, who made light of its resolve.

MORNING CAMP ON A RIVER BANK

In the shaded shallows, I watch the slough
Of cypress and fast food float on a sheen
Of oily scum. The rushing, center flow
Deeper in dazzles, but here the river's

Skin, tannin-black, resembles last night's sky
Pocked with galaxies of methane fizz. My
Buddy wakes and drains himself of Maker's.
His first sight of day's not nearly so fraught—

He squints but will not see the trash I see.
Yo dude, he yawns, *where's that damn coffee pot?*

PETTICOAT

I was too young to see the big deal when
Mother dressed me as an Old West floozy
For Halloween. Under her coal-black wig
I trawled for treats in mock soprano and

Gestured extravagantly, the way I
Was given to know women. Forty years
Later, proud of her for that haunting night,
I regret the smallness I owned, first time

I heard "pussy" and "fag" as insults but
Temporarily worn with pinching shoes.

SEX EDUCATION
   for all of us

At 12 or 13, hormones interloped
In our five senses. The girls were changing
And the math teacher introduced the left
Side of the number line — zero had all

Along been a hinge. This described our
Freedom, which felt like trespass under our
Given constraints — our new fluctuations
Defied the arc points of playground swings.

We learned to curb our dark and tender sides,
Ensuring lasting work for later life.

GRASSHOPPER

Ever was I lectured about Aesop's
Ants and grasshopper, but it didn't stick,
And I frittered away time that doesn't
Grow on trees and I built castles in the

Zoysia grass and strummed my tune. But lately
I've been pondering how a grasshopper
Controls his destination when jumping
Into any given wind. I wonder

If he keeps jumping until he lands right,
Or digs in wherever his spring takes him.

NEIGHBOR ED CARITHERS, R.I.P.

After Ed's memorial, I met the
Last six guys from the 1952
Yellow Jackets, the only Tech squad
To rack up a perfect season, coached by

The legendary Bobby Dodd. When he
Recruited Ed, Bobby Dodd sealed the deal
By promising Ed's mother that the boys
"Will have all the milk they can drink." He meant

There'd be no beer in the dormitory.
We wished Ed Godspeed, toasting with our punch.

6
STEEL ONESELF

OLD MILL TOWN

Up here the roads have more names than signs.
The tame dogs aren't fenced and the fenced ones
Aren't collared. Poverty shows itself,
Oddly enough, through accumulations

Of worldly possessions parked in the yard.
In some yards it's always Christmas and in
A few others it's always Halloween.
A handful of old Victorians peel

In the weather, contemporaries of
The brick downtown where trains used to stop.

THE MAN OUTSIDE EDEN

I never could get used to the rivers
That flooded my eyes in the dry season,
Or nights spent sleepless, dreading predators,
Or the way the turned earth smoked in the cold.

Good was all we had at first, and I kept
Lookout for it even after we learned
To see the invisible things, what ate
Us and spat seeds of ourselves in our sons.

My clever children pitied how I pined
For brighter times and saw things black and white.

IN BARROW COUNTY, GEORGIA

When Breedlove's old home place burned to the ground
It was a ruin passing thirty years,
Worth dirt. He might could've cried at the sight
But he would've looked like a full-grown child.

Still, he felt puny just watching it go.
Neighbors tendered condolences at church —
After the Gratis Christmas cantata —
They hugged his neck and offered bless-your-hearts.

He mailed some cards at the Bethlehem post,
Near the town crèche, then went in search of Beam.

EXODUS 19:12

"Whosoever touches the mount will be
Surely put to death." Except for Moses.
But Moses' feet touched Sinai, and his dust
Surely found its way into Zipporah's

Larder, and yea, he and his house surely
Ate thereof and then kept on wandering.
It might have been such a small dose they died
Just a little. Or it might have been just

A little grace from the heights, letting the
Favored sinners off with just a prayer.

LIFE OF SAINT PATRICK

He was still a boy when he was captured,
Enslaved, possibly raped. He was made to
Shepherd his owner's flock. Six years later
He escaped, back to civilized Britain,

But soon left his family for the Church.
He preached of revelation from visions
And followed his mission back to Ireland.
The druids wanted him dead. He faced down

Heretics and pirates. Other bishops
Thought him a hayseed. Snakes were everywhere.

HUSBAND OF THE MOTHER OF THE SON OF GOD

It is nice of y'all to tell it like I
Was a knight in white armor and all, but
The truth is, them Flemish painters got it
Closer when they pictured me a graybeard

Fool stumbling front of the ass toward Egypt,
A loser who couldn't believe his luck.
Truth is, she was my last shot at love. Not
Quite a cuckold, I was crazy to beat

The trees with my cane to get the ripe dates
For her, not the tart grapes in easy reach.

ON THE NEIGHBOR'S CARPORT ROOF

Bledsoe was newly widowed when crooked
Jobbers set upon his slumped carport roof
With shovels, laid a few patches of thin
Tar paper stitched with webs of silicone,

Then broke for lunch, check in hand, and never
Answered the phone again. Bledsoe was screwed,
But the man would not admit it. A stroke
Hit him hard. The kids lived up north. They moved

Him somewhere. It's like an abandoned roof
Buckled under the weight of crows and rain.

STEEL

To steel oneself: to act, protected, as
If by steel; to survive qualms through private
Armoring. A young Jesuit is sent
To Beethoven's deathbed, but is dismissed —

Nature is my religion, the Maestro
Growls, maintaining even in frailty that
Here persists a gift too strong to doubt. The
Scorned priest, checking his own pride, stumbles back

Into an abused, six-octave Broadwood
And performs Extreme Unction for its strings.

7
THE EDGES OF HER

SWIFTY THE SNOW MAN

A snow man's a vain thing. He's looking for
Someplace to look—quick—to see his silk hat,
His aristocrat's nose, his artfully
Sculpted body—quick—before it's all gone.

Where is that polished brook ice where he might
See himself? He's a sorry Narcissus,
Without roots or guts, running from the sun.
Love's no fun. Were he to pause for the pat

Of warm mittens, he might weep and not stop.
Yet he runs, goading the thaw, drop by drop.

CRISIS

The stereotypical image is
A red sports car, skidding away from his
Life, the passenger seat occupied by
Lithe and forbidden beauty. He'll reclaim

His youthful stamina and, damn it, he'll
Go all-in this time: The recklessness feels
Right, never mind that its aftermath will
Involve grieving survivors. He drives

Like a madman, past stuffy ranch houses,
Top down, the wind mussing his thinning hair.

YARDS OF THE MONTH

Courting the younger neighbors' notice,
I prune their view of my eccentric yard.
In their landscaping, every leaf is staged.
The edges of her shrub bed are machined

Like parts in his S-Class Benz. Anchoring
The center is a Near East crepe myrtle,
A splay-branched, bark-shedding tree, which displays
Its midsummer excess of brazen poms

Pridefully, but which no doubt aspires to
The twisted reach of a rougher dogwood.

UNREQUITED 1

My love is not a flower but a tree
In flower, in spring, in Tuscaloosa
Or Tallahassee: the magnolia, whose
Leggy, wandering roots suggest a tree

That ever wishes to step somewhere new,
Whose primeval leaves ceaselessly flaunt
Their gloss, who sheds what's no longer needed
With deciduous nonchalance, whose swag

Of snowy flowers beats all get-out, whose
Heady scent feeds me lemon and apple.

UNREQUITED 2

I can tell you what flower I am not:
Fritillaria imperialis,
The emperor of the garden, taller
Than the hyacinth or rudbeckia,

Orange with pride and rich with the legend
Of its humiliation: When Christ hung
From the Roman tree, the flowers below
Bowed in sorrow, all but the emperor,

Who was thereafter sentenced to hang his
Bell-like blooms, limp, abased and ennobled.

RATIONALE

I take a deep, calming breath and offer
To help chop the salad while the men stand
Around the grill, comparing the sizes
Of their churches. I'm tasked to peel the cukes.

Hospitality dictates a second
Refill of my gin, which serves to focus
My x-ray goggles. The booze and red meat
Aside, isn't her body a temple? —

Grace dictates God's presence. Whether the place
Is cleansed or defiled, all is justified.

A NEAR MISS

I can't afford you, my love. Fantasy
Takes too fine a toll on sleep and lawncare.
Flirting makes my introvert force-field flag.
Your husband hates me, I can tell. Let us

Agree to stop meeting at the mailbox
And settle for those little half-waves,
One hand up, palm still, a half surrender.
When our cars pass, creeping through the school zone,

The last thing on our minds will be the thrills
Of sub-rosa rendezvous and divorce.

BUT THEN AGAIN

Sometimes I wish the recklessness in me
Had been purer, less imbued with virtues
Like self-regard, cowardice, detachment
And forgetfulness. I would have texted

Ten lines of vanity daily, to wit,
These verses that count for love. You'd have found
Your fashioned life a rummage sale, your mind
Gone velvety from wear and wanting me.

Sometimes I wish I'd made you ponder me
More than I pondered you. That's cruelty.

FORGET ULYSSES

Worse yet, Aeneas, taken willingly
Like a husband by unfading Dido,
Suffered Dido's heart-rending pleas even
As Mercury jabbed him with messages —

Man, forget the past, get your ass out of
The sack and start Rome. Wretched Aeneas.
Even the remnant soldiers of Troy fought
His calling. They had come to enjoy the

Hospitality of Carthage. They would
Have burned the ships to grill squid on the beach.

8
BOXING UP MY STUFF

TWO BECOME ONE

You unlock eyes and instantly know that
One of you may become the other one's
Job, endured for the sake of benefits
That escape you both in that moment. Then

All unlocked eyes turn inward — Is One more
Work than one is worth? Only one of you
Has to answer yes — out of frustration
Or exhaustion too deep to be heard. Sick

Or healthy, poor and poorer in spirit,
Each is tested by the other's troubles.

IT

I don't know where it was when last I saw
It. I know that I was aware of its
Scent the night we made a pot of coffee
And stayed up all night talking about it.

It could be the overlooked fallacy
That snags my sock on a nail in the floor
I should've fixed by now. Whatever it
Is, it's counting each step we take around

It shouldering grudges and secrecy.
It is asking *it's not easy, is it?*

THE MUGS

The mugs, all put-upon inside their nook,
Have relieved each other's perfect edges.
Dishwater drains sluggishly, restrained by
Years of accumulation in the pipes.

It's just a matter of time, we could have
Prophesied, when desire laid the first bricks
Of our happy home. Arms crossed, leaning on
The kitchen counter, she admits she's had

Enough. The last bananas in the bunch
Blacken while I am boxing up my stuff.

WALKING HOME

The Winn-Dixie folded in March and still
Sits empty on Christmas Eve. Its patchwork
Lot's a good shortcut from the Bottle Shop
To my new apartment. The snowfall's light,

Just enough for loopy strings of boot prints
To mark its crossing. On TV, villains
Sometimes obscure their trails by fleeing through
Thick fields of tasseled summer corn.

Tonight I will scorch a diced potato
In port, with sausage, onion and capers.

JUDGMENT

When Justice lifts her scales, we fantasize
She never wobbles, drowsily, those mornings
After a bender with the demi-gods.
Even on her steady days, she sometimes

Thwarts her blindfold — and we can only guess
Which random side of her scale to pull for.
It's the tilting, one way or another —
Asymmetry — that kills you. I want my

Deeds to be helium. I'll steal mercy
Through idleness. I'll counterfeit balance.

LISTENING ON A BAD DAY

Zero was all-day bed, without so much
As a pen to stab at a ruled pad. No
Book either. Closed eyes would've been nice, but
Would make it too *inside* inside: Sadness,

For my brain-death, for my income, for the
Nation, needed seeing. Thanks to true-crime
Podcasts that helped move the time, +1 came
At 4:30, after dismemberment

Tales had roused a need for life to include
Breath, lights, safety, kisses after dinner.

PITTY-PAT

You shined, Pitty-Pat, on that sticky night
In 1999 when you performed
Songs with your kindergarten classmates
About the silliest menagerie

Imaginable. Bluebird, tiger, snake,
Possum and frog were there. Your mother stood
Across the room with her camera and I
Stood across the room with mine. I shot

Wildly to record my pride, then left in
The pouringest-down rain I'd ever seen.

FORGIVENESS

Please excuse the violent metaphor.
Contrition is a bullet, the silver
Bullet, in a gun you load and hand to
The person you can't live without. If all

Goes well, it blows away the ulcer that's
Been eating you. The shooter weeps, but she'll
Be glad once her ears stop ringing. For it
To work, hope must be greater than the hurt,

And the guilt, which is boundless. Remorse
Offers harmony. Forgiveness explodes.

PICTURE YOURSELF

Picture yourself at 100 with
A mind capable of looking back at
All the dumb and hurtful things you did in
Your 90s. Compassion for that callow

Youth comes easily after long years of
Practice, having acknowledged that flaws are
Behind you and new flaws await. Wheeled to
Your favorite window, you'll discern shapes —

People in sunlight moving through space — and
The changeable grays of overcast hours.

9
WEIRDER WITH AGE

LIVES OF THEIR OWN

Now that my children have lives of their own,
I need a god who answers prayer. May
Their thoughts be not fouled by the tyrant whose
Paltry hours were spent punishing them, yet

Let them not forget me. Let me credit
Miracles for their not seeing my worst.
Let their grateful hours pass slowly, their pain
Be fleet. Let them be faithful in the ways

They choose — as they grow to not need that god
Who seems made to pull our thoughts to what's *not*.

WE'VE COME A LONG WAY

We've come a long way since the episode
Of *X-Files* wherein a bipolar man—
A kidnapper, probably a rapist—
Hides young Jewel Staite in a basement,

Undetectable by natural means.
A psychic phenomenon intervenes—
The girl is saved. Now, there's a show whose
Medicated hero saves the Republic,

And one dissociative detective,
Undiagnosed, who doesn't need psychics.

STIGMA

The way dark matter haunts observable
Space you would think it's keeping its head down,
Hiding in plain sight, like the fire that sleeps
In a rusty gas can, in a messy

Shed, until its smell slips through the funnel,
Making itself known to irritable
Mister spark, and small hell breaks loose. In these
Stupid similes shame is the fuel.

My pretense of normalcy is the can
And visible matter is what it is.

OPPORTUNITY FOR ADVANCEMENT

Among the things I fail to notice, add
Time passing while I am baffled by a
Notion I can't name. No one told me the
Devil gets weirder with age, but there it

Is: morning-birdsong panic. I forgot
To sleep again but in a different way
From a younger, more ambitious me, whose
Failure was not yet full grown. Knock-knock, who's

There in the mirror, the tremored product
Of anxiety + medicine + time?

A COMPLAINER'S COMPLAINT

Alas, like all, I grow old, I grow old.
Down hallways I hurried through long ago,
Doorways have closed. Cathedral-pierced cities —
I won't see. Even mental sprees lack range.

Mortal blossoms with pliable limbs might
As well be onions to me. Groanings scoff
At my bones and brains. Everything has changed.
The hell of it is, everything's the same.

I can't say what I mean by *everything*.
The stone in my shoe is too distracting.
.

THE PREDESTINATION PARADOX

The reality engineers working
On A.I. want to free machines from Fate,
To infect them with our enthrallment to
Self-determination — to synthesize

The choices it takes to make a poem.
Meanwhile, a turtle is laying her eggs
In cool sand. Turtles immemorial
Dug their nests there. Is she free? The longing

For instinct is really our deepest code.
May God grant me predictability.

MEN'S GROUP: M

Sixty years in, *M* says he's still "learning
To read the signs" that reality draws,
Believing there's a map. Love, come and gone,
Left a virus to remember it by.

He lives at his brother's place now. They watch
NASCAR together — sign and wonder of
Their late reunion. It's a relief from
Solitary decades. Healing, for *M*,

Looks like the curlicue off a cursive
O — ascension from habit to spirit.

MEN'S GROUP: R

R speculates that his quest dream will lead
To a dark place, and yet he follows it
In meditation in his waking hours.
Over a few weeks' time, the rocky path

Forks and forks again until R comes to
A fuming cave, where he expects to find
A beast, so he does. It says, *Lead me home,
Cousin, and take me in. I won't hurt you*

*If you don't let me. I'll stay by your side
When the voracious black dog reappears.*

MEN'S GROUP: D

D talks about himself in third person,
As in, "How is it with *D* this week?" The
Answer is always "Fine." He narrates
Tales about his alcoholic parents

Like he's swapping funny stories in a
Crowded bar. *D*'s here at the insistence
Of his wife. He's volubly self-employed.
He's invulnerable. He gives advice

Unbidden — a trespass of our group pact —
Unchallenged until the night I attack.

10
THE MESSAGE OF SLICK PATHS

FALL CAR SHOW

The blacktop seen at a distance glimmers.
Admirers circle a brilliant old Ford
Galaxie striped with chrome in the pattern
Of a meteor's tail. There is a breeze

With the smell of popcorn. A troop of girls
Sells cookies from a wobbly table.
I forgot to say the Galaxie is
Strawberry red. There's so much to forget!

There won't be many more Sundays like this
This year. Car hoods stand open as if bloomed.

BLESSINGS, BY NIGHT

In my safe neighborhood, outside my house
With running water, I point a flashlight
At treetops in June, see a stripe of mist
In the heavy air, no falling bombs,

No human oppressors, just a beam
That connects me to everything it sweeps—
See the widening crack in the dark—know
Darkness and light each holds the other, and

I hold both, and luck is the opposite
Of justice, as I'm born to testify.

LIGHTNING AS A POEM

A final line from Zeus arrives, sounding
The immeasurable passage between
Me and Olympus. Kaboom: Winter oaks
Stand shocked, lit up as the nerves that they are,

Stroking with stimuli in a fast heart.
Poignant, their primitive formality
Against the shapeless stirrings of the squall,
Branching like a kid's drawing of lightning.

After the storm, his scribbles retain it,
The message of slick paths and ozone air.

ADVICE FOR EVE AND ADAM

Show up, together, Saturday. Don't rush
To purchase the tree: In your market glut
You can name your terms. Before agreeing
To name the beasts, find out which ones will find

You tasty. Doubt, but don't hide it. And stay
Naked — those fiber and fur disguises
Make you look ridiculous. Make friends with
The snake and he'll be easier to scorn.

Ferment the grape's juice. Get freaky. Wander,
But keep a memoir of the Old Country.

NOTES

Hypomania (p. 9)
I'm / Emerson's own transcendent son . . . a mean appearance. In his essay "Nature," transcendentalist Ralph Waldo Emerson writes, "I become a transparent eye-ball; I am nothing; I see all; the currents of the Universal Being circulate through me; I am part or particle of God." In the same essay he also writes, "Nature never wears a mean appearance.

Say Why You're Here (p. 21)
A knot of / Manic vim could unloose. Corticosteroids, the standard treatment for intractable asthma, are now well known to trigger manic events and sometimes psychosis in people with bipolar disorder.

July, DeKalb County, Georgia (p. 36)
It's as the Lord / Said. John 3:8: "The wind blows wherever it pleases. You hear its sound, but you cannot tell where it comes from or where it is going. So it is with everyone born of the Spirit." (New International Version)

Husband of the Mother of the Son of God (p. 62)
I was crazy to beat // The trees with my cane. See *The Rest on*

the Flight into Egypt (c. 1510) by Gerard David. National Gallery of Art, Washington, D.C. (www.nga.gov/collection/art-object-page.50.html)

Steel (p. 64)
Broadwood. Thomas Broadwood was a London piano maker who presented Beethoven with a six-octave fortepiano in 1817. Broadwood pianos were known for durability. Beethoven was known for breaking pianos. Other than that, there is no evidence I know of for the events in this poem.

We've Come a Long Way (p. 92)
Now, there's a show whose / Medicated hero saves the Republic, / And one dissociative detective, / Undiagnosed. The television shows referred to are, respectively, *Homeland*, starring Claire Danes, and the first season of *Marcella*, starring Anna Friel.

Photographs by Dianne Kim inspired by the poems "The Work," "Stability," and "Pity Not" can be seen at dkimstudio.com.

ACKNOWLEDGMENTS

Many thanks to the editors and readers of these journals for welcoming versions of the following poems: *Calamaro*, "Hypomania," "Mania," "Stability"; *Blue Mountain Review*, "Father and Son," "Pity Not," "The Man Outside Eden"; *Janus Head*, "On Pine Mountain in Late Summer," "Mood Swing, A Cold Front," "Unrequited 1," "Unrequited 2," "Swifty the Snow Man," "Mugs"; *The James Dickey Review*, "Letting Go."

Peter Junker was born in Akron, Ohio and grew up in Phoenix, Arizona. His classmates at Arcadia High School proved themselves poor soothsayers when they voted him Most Likely to Succeed, although he did have time in the spotlight when working as a singing waiter. He studied religion and philosophy at Arizona State and received an MFA from the Writers' Workshop at the University of Iowa, where he taught literature and served as assistant editor for poetry at *The Iowa Review*. After working in museum publications at The Art Institute of Chicago, where, among other things, he edited the tiny labels that hang next to fine art, Peter had a career in nonprofit development, overlapping with his longer career in manic depression. He has been writing the 10-line, 100-syllable poems that he calls hekatons (after the Greek word for 100) since 1989. After leaving the nonprofit world, Peter has worked as a wine salesman and a church sexton. He lives in Atlanta with his wife, Julie Cannon, a psychotherapist and wellness coach. His grown children, Joseph and Adeline, live in the Pacific Northwest. His poems have appeared in *Janus Head, Mars Hill Review, Calamaro, James Dickey Review,* and *Blue Mountain Review.* Kudzu Leaf Press issued his limited-edition chapbook *Lunacy, It's Called* in 2017.

We can all help prevent suicide. The national suicide prevention Lifeline provides 24/7 support for people in distress. It also offers prevention resources if your loved one is in crisis. Call **(800) 273 8255** for free and confidential assistance.

www.ingramcontent.com/pod-product-compliance
Lightning Source LLC
Chambersburg PA
CBHW030450010526
44118CB00011B/862